D1460875

Pluto

GLYN MAXWELL has won several awards for his poetry, including the Somerset Maugham Prize, the E. M. Forster Prize from the American Academy of Arts and Letters and the Geoffrey Faber Memorial Prize. His work has been shortlisted for the Whitbread, Forward and T. S. Eliot Prizes. Many of his plays have been staged in the UK and USA, including *The Lifeblood*, which won British Theatre Guide's 'Best Play' Award at the Edinburgh Fringe in 2004, and *Liberty*, which premiered at Shakespeare's Globe in 2008. He recently published *On Poetry*, a general reader's guide to the craft.

Glyn Maxwell

Pluto

PICADOR

First published 2013 by Picador
an imprint of Pan Macmillan, a division of Macmillan Publishers Limited
Pan Macmillan, 20 New Wharf Road, London N1 9RR
Basingstoke and Oxford
Associated companies throughout the world
www.panmacmillan.com

ISBN 978-1-4472-3158-5

9 8 7 6 5 4 3 2 1

A CIP catalogue record for this book is available from the British Library.

Printed and bound by CPI Group (UK) Ltd, Croydon, CR0 4YY

Contents

Pluto

The Byelaws

Never have met me, know me well,
tell all the world there was little to tell,
say I was heavenly, say I was hell,
harry me over the blasted moors
      but come my way, go yours.

Never have touched me, take me apart,
trundle me through my town in a cart,
figure me out with the aid of a chart,
finally add to the feeble applause
      and come my way, go yours.

Never have read me, look at me now,
get why I'm doing it, don't get how,
other way round, have a rest, have a row,
have skirmishes with me, have wars,
      O come my way, go yours.

Never have left me, never come back,
mourn me in miniskirts, date me in black,
undress as I dress, when I unpack pack
yet pause for eternity on all fours
      to come my way, go yours.

Never have met me, never do,
never be mine, never even be you,
approach from a point it's impossible to
at a time you don't have, and by these byelaws
      come my way, go yours.

South-East of Eden

Together they took the least space they could.
Entered each other deeply, to be less,
to throw one shadow only, to be still
for all the world while moving for each other.

So space, so barely dented, might not bruise
and cry, and time come running. This was why
their breaths were held inside till the only end
of that – this side of nothing – the great sigh
that gives the place away . . .
                              And out they come,
exiting one another with the kiss
to heal the bruise and be the bruise and there
they sit. The only angel in this case
came only there to point them, in their first
amazing silence, to two peaceful desks.

The Ages

Let's get this straight. It may be fairly said
that yes I roamed the earth when you were not.
That yes I had my small talk with the dead
and wept to hear some President got shot
trying to enjoy the play. For sure my world
had wars in it and peace and far and wide
I sauntered – all the stories you were told
have me in them somewhere, off to the side.
But all the stuff I know has you somewhere.
And I've been trying to do this since half-four.
So all that to and fro means nothing more
to me than time I took and time I make,
yawning and fretting in this garden chair,
whiling away the ages till you wake.

No Special Day

It has asked to be treated like all the other days.
Not to be beamed at in assembly,
winked at, singled out for praise,
parted for or crowded round, not to be
starred or handed a badge or in obvious ways

made something of. In no uncertain terms
did it say no gifts, no cake, no fuss,
no speeches, hugs, and christ no poems.
Look how I've answered what it asked of us.
Touched, it gently frees itself from my arms.

My Talk

I never did quite get round to the poem for you.
I mean I never got round to the poem for her.
I was going to write one, I fully intended to.
I guess we were busy being what we were.

And whoever's trailing me out to the end of this line
probably doesn't think he or she has need
of a guide to tour these ruins, would be just fine
alone with earphones or a sheet to read

abstractedly in the lemon-grey sunrise.
And he or she would be right. In fact right now
I can see he and she: they are meeting each other's eyes
and edging away from my talk, they have met somehow

by mutual mouthing of the sweet *so what*,
no more to say, their attitudes agree
as they drift together away in the dust while you lot
stay to the end, which means the world to me.

Dunwich

Not even old, I've stories I've stopped telling.
Can't say for sure which girl they were told to.
Girls. I dine, I wonder where the gang went.
And *you*

means what? The months go by and you go by –
brunette, petite, licentious, lippy, young –
tick any three from those but you go by,
someone,

while like a patient I lie reading here
between the lamps that bob towards, away
into and out of darkness they make dark (you
don't say)

and I know where this is heading as I've seen
the skilled old lady in her lab, I've seen her
slice the fawn mille-feuilles of a new brain
'just in'

she let me hold and you could see the problem.
Erosion like East Angular . . . It's water
fills the spaces, water seeks to make it
better,

hopes it always will, like prayer to swim in.
Women. And I wonder where the gang went.
I think of calling you but I did that, you
didn't

answer, why *would* you when you don't know
which girl you were? It's water seeks to make it
better, fills the space. When we next meet
we meet

at church in Dunwich, under the blue briny
drifting to our hopes. Seen from the heights
as by the skilled old lady in her lab
these lights

of Sunday coalesce as a white core,
while on the fringes blots of red and green,
outlying cottages you can imagine
life in

and stories being told in, go out.
A violet echo-image blooms and nothing
now. The months go by and you go by.
Something

stops. I wake, I wonder where the gang went.
Meet me on Monday, you, at the marketplace.
Never have met me, know me well, be no one
else.

The Drummers

I thought how it might go between us (love,
this is) where *us* referred to two real people,
and after it didn't go that way at all
I thought how someone time has never heard of

might just – appear. When nothing of the kind
transpired and no one of the kind came by,
I fed that story through me anyway
with you. Now every scene that sprung to mind

was doomed for sure – as if my every thought
was what the other side had been in training
day and night to spot, a column forming,
imperial scarlet sweating by a fort,

some regimental yell and down they fall,
the drummers. They knew nothing but the step
demanded, plus the usual stuff they hope,
yanked from a pocket, soiled and legible.

The Net

for Caryl Phillips

It booted up and everyone you guessed
would be there *was* – on bunks, on babel-towers
of bunks, five to a bunk, shelved, legs dangling
homeward like the mischievously munching
dead on that high girder over midtown.
There was no room for everyone there was room for.
Noise were it not intolerable silence
would have been unbearable noise, it was all sepia
thank god till you remembered it was sepia
you chose. No one to thank but you, no one
to blame but you or choose but you. You tried
to close in on one face to make it blurry
but it sharpened like a sniper. Next you tried
to zoom the fuck away and you got the Earth.

Pluto

Life in the care of memory is story.
Right around Christmastime it's Christmas story.
But I wake on a white sheet: January. If Christmas
comes now then I get it, it's a miracle.

But February does, to the still alive, a sour
official at your side, he is on your side,
he never believed it really. He is dying
to confide in you he never believed it really.

Alfie turns twelve in March and that's all she wrote.
To say she's like this or is this, like we do in poems,
strikes me as time I could be in Sussex with her,
trampolining. Most things strike me as that.

On God I abstain like a poet. I do do Easter.
You are all, to the back teeth, paralysed in traffic
outside Emmaus, soon to be disabused
of the reasonable assumption that I'm dead now.

April's the blonde in a determined girl-band,
a daisy-chain of iPods: they went solo.
May was as undecided as she sounded.
June I would snog in a heartbeat, pausing only

to think about it. Where the hell did *she* go?
Where the hell did they *all* go? Where did *I* go?
I am looking for something I had for a week in July
not last July this is but during the Cold War.

August went *hey man* so I went hey man,
anything going down later? And we just smoked
and trod our shadows. One of us said *those chicks
were really hot* I've a horrible feeling I did.

September is trying to empathise with pain
it causes. Everyone's old and everyone's new.
Someone in English says there's a star in the east!
Next morning you ask in Maths and he says it's a plane.

What you are going to have to endure one day
will come like a skull or a witch or a web or a ghost.
It will look like Halloween doesn't half start early
but it's actually last year's one metastasizing

gaily. Cue November the Seventh, all
I mean by miracle. That I up and made it.
My other great date I can honestly say I've not met.
She lives at the end of the line and has no small talk.

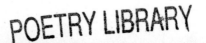

The years are clattering in from the icy fields
with what they've got. The first three next to nothing;
the next three three dumb furry things that are all
they loved; the next three? gifts you're kind of stuck with,

and all of the rest bring everything that's left
and hoist it high towards the glow. December's
welcome to this scene, the souls in circles
widening out into darkness warming each other,

thinking the glow does that when the glow does jack
but show you where to stare. And when I one day
find myself in a crush like that I'll hate it,
I'll elbow out to the edge where the light is gone

like the sun for Pluto, like that morning Pluto
learned it was not a planet so I took Pluto
out for some ales with everyone I've forgotten
in a dive so deep in the earth I knew you all.

The Case of After

Affair. Always over. Even starting
don't call it that unless you know it's nothing
in the great scheme of things what scheme of things.

None of them were affairs. The pretty tour-guide
by the cemetery goes none of this lot were dead.
I wait for her to run with that, I wait

for them to. All it is is Time is crossed
like a kingpin, who is signalling, with kisses,
love for you, instructions for the bruisers.

The old guy likes a wedding-day, a contract,
things signed in books he likes though he himself
will be selecting clubs on a very private

links when he is told you know that thing
they signed? they never signed. He takes his swing.
Everyone winces skyward and starts clapping.

Affairs. Always over. Even starting
don't call it that unless you know it's nothing.
These came before the only vows I made

in my long life and after I unmade them.
Ten years between we sailed with his sort of blessing.
Tears in his eyes he even gave us something

nothing can take back, a perfect time-piece.
When he comes visiting he's pleased as Punch
to see a child, but that's as close to peace

as he can make with us. The front door's closing.
That went well I think. Then I heard running.
Putting the plump white album back there's something's

fallen out and isn't meant to be there.
Drawers are stiff with things not meant to be there.
They go where stuff that isn't meant to be there

goes, like here – she and I, no her and me,
dative, done to, parked her car by country
inns we didn't know because nobody

needs to, quite like now, and we spent our nights
like a share in winnings, biffing the pale sheets
in eight directions like the Bash Street Kids

hoist by their mischief. I wrote 'Watching Over'
about you and was blissfully aware
I am writing this and it will still be here

now and you wouldn't. *Blissfully aware*
is more than an oxymoron, a matched pair
outstaring amiably till we don't care:

blissfully aware is a little clownfish
gliding through the pearly teeth. Where are you?
I became aware we were done and no one knew

we'd ever been. I looked at you for a look
to guide me at some party – there's a book
when I was small in an old library nook

I leafed it to a page I jumped my skin
to have face-time with Struwwelpeter, wan
death-headed wight and worse was Scissor-Man –

and the odds against my brain erasing them
are the odds against it wiping out the look
you gave me. *Odi et amo* fine but *fuck*

you were gone, so gone the creatures that are gone
were at the door saying Glen you know us, man,
we got some cans of Stella let us in mate.

You and I, accusative – like it matters
in English – someone else, I mean, some other
case, some other party, someone's sofa.

We couldn't *do* this so we did all summer
and then some earlier summer. It was over
loads of times, it was always nearly over,

there had never been anything like it several times
and Time, alerted by those loyal hoodlums
indignant at the nerve of these crimes

pissed himself laughing. The old guys joined in.
The old guys then the new guys joined in.
They were henchmen, they join in, they laughed so long

what's funny. Nothing. Time said *Do it then.*
We were pouring pinot noir in N1.
Next morning we never saw each other again

and haven't yet. Where are you? Yours and mine
(I've moved on) *mine*, the genitive, *you are mine*
is a phrase I cherished only when I'd moved on

and couldn't use it. Then I kind of craved it.
Bored researchers timing a lab-rat
showed more surprise than you at my saying that.

We ordered. And I'd smudged the dear white sky
with carbon to ask this of you. Things die
when I do this. Time stands innocently by

when I spin the wheel myself. O look at that
he yawns, and lights go off along my street
months later as I spool the best of it

like a teaser on my eyelids: chase, kiss,
what used to be passed X, and that bass voice
from trailers: *THIS IS NOT THE THING THAT IS*

like a Hollywood Houyhnhnm. That you get that stuff
through a gateway called Yahoo I'm well aware of
and I do try not to but not hard enough.

Then we did it all again after I wrote this.
Wasted each other's time like we were sponsored.
Got scammed together, filled a rascal's coffers.

Then we did it all again after that *last* line.
Saw eye to eye for nothing, like the last time.
This wasn't the last time either, that was the next time.

Where are you? What's that other case we don't have.
Ablative, from which, in which, means of,
manner, agent, instrument of. Love

observes things working in mysterious ways
and is curious why they do that when it's easy.
Tiptoeing up the Thames is if you're Jesus.

I decided it was easy on a laptop,
love – in point of fact this very laptop,
on which I spend my days you can see I've cracked it.

She wore dark glasses in the only photo
I could access yet. I was peering at that window
like Peter sodding Quint I had the blue glow

on me, she was someone in the City,
and I was not, together would be easy,
a perfect sum quite calculably lovely,

and she went by Notthefaintest and I went by
damned if I'll tell you lot. By the way,
Notthefaintest, said I wrote poetry

didn't I, *Lynn*. Not her real name, I mean
her real name on the site but not her name
probably when she's sleeping. I gave my name

as honestly as I'll speak when the padre murmurs
Do you take Notthefaintest? Christ yes.
She had this exquisite jawline and her clothes

were cool and the sky was blue when she posed for that.
We sent some messages, Lynn & Greg, made a date
in Notting Hill, a real place till they made

Notting Hill about it. Now my dreams
at least began with her, like most films
at least begin with life. My Houyhnhnms

look on impassively as I leave my flat,
two hours in hand to go on a first date
convinced somebody I have never met

and never would (she texted me some shite
about her kid being ill and I had to write
I hope he gets better soon while harbouring doubts

he was ever born) anyway, sure *that*
was the shortcut to it all. Time the slum-lord
sees no harm in that, there being a kid

involved an' all, have a tenner, water under.
Men of business watching an East End vicar
trotting down some empty street, a trooper

that boy, a real trooper, true believer
with bollock-all to go on, makes yer wonder
don't it just? and they clink four pints together,

wondering sweet f.a. My history now
and England in the afternoon, the morning
coffee in my system and the evening

bottle on my mind – I'm not the one
tour-guided through a garden stone by stone:
when your faces float across, stone's what I am.

To you I was what I was, there was no more
to know, I am written down. A faintest tone
of poor endeavour and a stranded song

might cling like moss a while to my inscription
but one moves on and you are all that one.
The pathway's not so long you'd turn again,

and not so wide you even could. Were there
more, not a future tense but a *case* of After,
this I would take to be its atmosphere:

grey skies, no rain, now everything's gone by,
'Love' 'Hate' 'Forgiveness' prints from the old country,
puzzling us as we press on all day,

tireless in that slow descending spiral
Escher just dashed off with a special pencil
Time's asking where he got. All those I've mentioned

walk this with me nowadays now Time
is through with us. I walk the wet street home
vaguely protected, vaguely known to him,

and not in life not yet but in this poem
you're in my way with coffees you can't manage,
so I splay my hand against a door to solve that

and your hair's tied back like someone's was at playtime
and we've not a clue which one of us got chatting
but we do have seven in-jokes by the next time,

when the light on Upper Street could be either dusk
or dawn, seeing as nothing now is over,
though, diligent as shadows to each corner,

hurry the foot-soldiers young and old,
who say down cell-phones nobody is holding
Clocked 'em boss, or, as we pass them, nothing.

This Whiteness

for Ann Kjellberg

This whiteness followed me at the speed of dawn.
A life-form in the fingers of an avalanche
I was, I was motion caught, I was a spot
found out by white, some foe of it, some germ

at frantic speed. The day sips its gluhwein,
high above in the tinkling chalet, stuffed,
beside the fire and betting on my chances –
who? down in the valley somewhere, blue now.

Gone, I begin again. Such is the motto
stamped on me by whiteness I enrage
by naming anything. That I only *breathe*
by naming I attempt to call my credo –

and see, the whiteness slashed me like a creature.
Stock-still I wait. They stash in these little stanzas
welcome rations, but the thing's outside,
pawing the air and pitiless with hunger.

Gone, I begin again. In the lovely village
every morning's Christmas, and the shops
out-glisten nature. Nobody's from here.
Enormous empty boots line up, the average

girl is an angel trying some on. An *angel*.
I ran from a word like that but I didn't make it.
I made this shelter, I, and she doesn't know it.
I won't be there when she turns, typical angel,

time her own. I went, I began again –
it's only the quest of the cold thing for the warm thing,
vowels to soften all, she cups hot chocolate
outside The Blue Grill, freezing in the sunshine,

and I think of Brodsky saying that for a *star*
to love its neighbour – there's where the big idea
was had, such were the distances it travelled . . .
He made that out of words, but he lived there,

when one great desert left him to another,
twice. She ties her boots. What *I* mean by angel
is one who comes from nowhere to reveal
there's nowhere else but now it doesn't matter.

She looks at where I was, then cools her gaze
as the hooded happy groups go slushing by
towards the hut that sends them to the mountain.
When I glance back from the peaks around, her place

is taken by some family and I'm
bereft like she was everything. The young
go sailing overhead, they're all like them.
To not go up, to come this far from home

for nothing earns a stripe from the whiteness. We,
it and I, will spend the day alone
and dazzled in this blinding bright valhalla,
writing postcards from it we're unlikely

to send until we're gone, if ever. The sunlight
gave like a billionaire and falls like one,
in just an hour with red signs switching on
in every language till it's out of sight.

The line of empty boots is back, the angel
nowhere to be seen but the old station,
posted there with all the past forbidden.
I saunter back with whisky to my table

and see the whiteness left its card. Evening.
The snow's the blue of being not a thing
that ends, while empty chair after empty chair
swing round the mechanism and keep going.

Agamemnon Home

Agamemnon, home from how it was,
his name enormous and unlike his things
impossible to set down in the old dust,
set himself down on a bench in the old dust,
surveyed the last road home.

A concubine, as all the world predicted,
stood yawning. Then, as no one but Cassandra
foresaw, sat and held his hand for ages.
He looked at her and she was the slim height
she was. The bench they sat on

was a sailboat and distance was the ocean.
Perspective ended here for Agamemnon.
When dusk came the beacons men had lit
to bring the news of Troy were lit matches,
the nearest man a tick

made on a list of dead men. Troy itself
was a toy lost in a garden, once remembered
in old age with a shiver some sweet nurse
thinks is 'flu. As night fell, the beacons
lit to bring the news

grew brighter, were the pearls on the birthday necklace
of a daughter, they belonged in a timeless circle
round her neck and not in that loosened string
that dwindled to the horizon. His Cassandra
saw the past had come.

The Window

In memory of Matthew Burrows

Back at a desk I steer the thing through time.
In time I slide a drawer of photos out
to accelerate the star-ship
then slide it in and shut.
Doing either seems to do the same.

What's the destination when the window's
all I ever come to? My first schooldays
are mornings for a month
till the little place advises
he's too young and helps me from their window

home again, which is what I was hoping for.
All I was hoping for. To be happened on,
clocked by one outdoors,
misting a window-pane,
four eyes on time, a wish to wish no more.

These mornings at the screen, when all that's been
is voices streaming in the room behind –
all the settled children –
this face is to be found
afloat on glass again, shy second son

of what's to come. – Somewhere on a toll-road
my house comes into view where no one lives,
then as you're slowing by
you glimpse me, but your lives
go on, you never end, the tales you heard

about me are the case, the joke you told
dead-on but you drive on, say that's *that* done
and zoom away. This face
is with you like the moon
is with the world when day is with the world.

*

Top of the list my daughter I just spoke to
an hour ago, texting from her school-day.
Then pals, appointments, agents
next, the girl from Sunday,
then scroll, scroll to the last name, you, Matthew.

I could delete it in a moment briefer
than moments used to be but I just don't.
It says let's get together
last Christmas but I couldn't
and the next news of you was the last ever.

Years went out like that. And though I'd walk
not one step of the steep devoting journey
you walked, still I'd let
time go by like money
till I sat in rows with hundreds of the broke,

needing to pay yet being asked for nothing.
So I must have believed something, to have let
your dear, deep, chuckling
time flow out like that,
must have believed our afternoons of boozing

and women-talk and Dylan tracks were days
available hereafter. I felt found
in your company, I felt lost
like one who'll still be found
however far he sails, steered by grace

and maybe I was just that middle son
afraid of it, who knows what's through the door
but makes his answer wrong
so he won't have to go there.
He clocks the street instead in a daze of sunshine.

*

In a moment briefer than a thought I send
'this afternoon you will be with me in paradise'
but Google rolls its eyes:
not 'afternoon' – it says
'day' in each result. But in the spellbound

shade of the wings of our stage at infant school,
gawping at Calvary (in the wings as God,
a good actor like my mum,
a good speaker like my dad)
it's 'afternoon' I heard and I hear still,

as if *that* afternoon, *this* afternoon
was what He meant, home-time with everyone
arriving, someone loved
to walk with, to be gone,
to walk till home is all of the horizon

and the world sits on the window-sill again.
Thirty thousand afternoons, the golden
and the grey. I am home now
thinking of you, with Dylan
singing of you, pages, wine, and no one.

What I can't believe about what you believed —
is scarcely more incredible than *Time*,
sweet, storied, generous,
cold, pitiless and dumb,
till I wonder if I'm loving what you loved,

mate, in my own way, at my window-pane.
I don't think so but I don't think anything.
Alfie texts me something
now, from school, while I'm writing,
and I beam at her on a tiny grey-lit screen.

*

I do think things. I think the whole of science
waits. Astonishment, the infant's blink,
made way for recognition
every bit as blank.
O the mouth opens. Only, when it opens

it opens at this window, for old words
in new deployments, verse as separate
from other verse as what,
a pane of glass rained-at
from its neighbour-pane of glass rained-at. The words

dry the same and stay the same. The view
is of a person listening, not now,
not now, listening someday
to tales from long ago. –
One yellow endless afternoon with you

you mention Levinas, philosopher,
his 'eyes of the Other' – infinite and gentle –
and I'm not sure that that isn't
all we ever meant,
all we ever roared about and lived for.

And this is what I do with time without it.
The rains stream down the window, they do,
in your beloved London
in the future, Matthew,
as I write about it all I know about it,

that Other, and it's no surprise the space,
my whiteness, starts to brighten like snow,
sunlit snow and my eyes
turn aching from the window,
to see what time has scribbled in my place.

The Given

Only you could make my years without you
seem a thing I meant.
Like gifts I'd chosen, wrapped for you and left
without comment.

Because your answer's this unasking quiet,
as if to show me how
they give a gift where you come from, or where
you are now.

Your quiet goes with His, you get your mile-high
Y. Now you can be
like Him to me when I was small, the light
alight for me,

the given. And my witless years without you
bustle to me as if
they happened to be passing, somehow
have time enough

to make a date: the little Christmas diaries
flutter on each palm
as they peck for light and I don't have the heart
to tell them.

Greenwich

At Greenwich we convene, sweet Time and I,
long having been each other's only subjects,
for a game of noughts-and-crosses just close by

the old Date Line. She fixes her first X
while adding *You are done for if you dare* –
and O's the only figure my mouth makes

in the face of that, though in this game it's fair,
my point's allowed but her next X is saying
north south east or west you exit here –

oh I'll Oblige, I go, when I'm done playing!
She puts that to the sword with two deft strokes
I realise mean *Sex* but I'm replying

already with my O for Love! *No jokes*,
she sniffs at that, pretends to go along
then suddenly game over – *meet your Ex* –

and I wonder how I got this match so wrong
that neither space could win for me – I cry
Let's play again! But Time is moving on

towards some texting kids who'd like a try.
Home I stroll from Greenwich, my last O
a seeing how, short of a seeing why.

Stephaton

Up come the longing hands
in the late day,
binding a nib with rags
and raising in air
the ungainly stick to the mustering
clouds above.

Like a lighter of lamps it
trembles; nothing's lit,
but it bobs on high in the dark
a trickling sponge,
towards which ever wound it was
just said something.

Longinus

I remember the sky so dark
and light at once
it was like a door kept banging,
and into a room
that stayed completely empty they
kept on coming.
I opened my eyes, there was us
in our brass togs
below the preposterous object
of all attention.
I determined to be the only one
with my sights trained
instead on the cold horizon.
But it reached us,
that horizon, wound around each
figure standing
gaping, arms by his sides, stupid,
included. I,
for them, was about to do something
I had to, raise
the diagonal into this dumb
standoff, something
to climb by, up by, something to show Him
my true colours.
And that was the deadlock broken.
He said His piece
I said mine, I meant nothing more
than I am His,
because I am anyone's who can make
me do this.

Christmas Seven Times Seven

Seven-times-seven of these
till now, one spent alone.
I watch first lights come on
on a houseboat by the dim canal.
There are two whole families
somewhere on the earth I'll call
who wouldn't be surprised.

Seven-times-seven of these.
I woke up eye to eye
with my little zombie tree
whose blue-green-crimson bulbs still light
a path through other trees
to the beckoning unearthly spot
if I thin my eyes and think so.

Seven-times-seven. Today
falls on a Saturday,
like a tramp who's trying to say
it's Saturday to the holy beaming
family riding by,
their tinsel tied and fluttering,
their kindness claiming *his* kind

though seven-times-seven times
in fifty times they leave him
wordless by a dustbin.
The early light is pale and tinted,

precious, this one time
I've nothing much to bring it
but our old words for numbers.

Seven-times-seven breaths
and something comes, as if
the dark won't stand for it,
silence can't endure it either –
whatever breathes *time* breathes
and that abiding something-other
holds me like what holds those who

these seven-times-seven years
have clustered to their eerie
consolatory short story
that's everything a child *would* hope:
that a time comes, reappears,
that with a firm and measured step
it's all at once beside us

like seven-times-seven footsteps
along the sounding tunnel
as I walk this old canal.
And as often as I turn to see
who's there and they're my steps,
I think they're mine till somebody
goes past me without turning.

Creature of a Play

She sleeps out of this world and wakes in earshot
of nothing she can understand. The place
is forest-brown resolving into sunlight,
the time this sound.

Which bounces between voices but to her
is one, or she adores it like it's one,
or she adores it like it's come for her
or it's come back

some way she knew it would. She only knows
it's all she wants whatever were the causes.
Out jumps breath, her breaths, she didn't know
she kept them there

till now they're all she has and what she's hearing
lasts with them like notes as long as air
is human. She is going where it's going,
that moment on,

treading forward to the gate of earshot,
into earshot, drawn whole into story,
into scene and line and plot and secret,
men and women

brutally illuminated, whole,
but evolving as she stares and sees them – *Eyes*
loom up to light a path, all will be well,
one mouth decrees

in terror, walls are pounded for her sake –
Away she runs so fast the dead are heated
back to life a second, apoplectic
as they fade

The Double

I made a dance and called it after you.
It was called The Double [here's where your surname went].
My arms go out as if about to be lifting
heavy bags, I stoop as if to do that,
then rise and smile, approach a facing partner
who's doing what I'm doing, bearing nothing,
forearms trailing downward like a scarecrow's,
and then we just link up and go round and round
as if there never were bags and it all dissolves
into the night. I didn't really know you.

Which is why it was odd you showed up at my folks'
when I'd left for university. They beamed
politely unclear who you were and then and there
you performed the original Double [surname here]
and stayed for a week. I'd been a month at Oxford
when you tracked me down one day. I would dine out,
dancing the Double [you] for years after,
on the basis of the afternoon you sat there
in my spacious digs and steadily described
how the city streets were dense with 'the evil people'
monitoring you. Many of them were airborne.
I was not equipped for anything but laughing,
though solemnly pretending to believe you
was fun too, now I think. When you next came –
it not having crossed my mind to call a doctor –
you said you had 'good' inside you, you had power now,

you could defeat them, you held a little match flame
twenty seconds and out it went, and not
because flames do, but because you compelled it to.
That was your power. I smiled the smile of someone
already planning who to tell this thing to?
For the story had some balance now, I remember
jotting it down in a book when you'd wandered off,
all evil vanquished one November lunchtime
and me the first to know. I got down to writing.
And I heard you got married one year, and I even saw you
act in a play back home with your new name
set bright between your old names like a shield.
I even laughed at that, like your enemy.

You were not the first or the last to remind the gents
responsible for housing psychotic patients
on the sixth floor of the hospital why they shouldn't.
You were the year below me. Needless to say
I never danced the dance again or enjoyed
telling the tale again. There *were* evil people.
Some of them really could fly. You had good inside you.
You did make the match go out. You made me make
a dance of my supreme indifference,
then a poem of my useless sorrow.

Birthplace

Hard to remember, now there is nothing here,
that there was once nothing here. Hard to remember
they paused in a field with a plot for a field and a feel
of a place in mind and a little knot of horses
    faraway in a corner stood there

pretty much where that little knot of horses
stands. The railway ran through the white template,
the life and death of it, made east and west
of nowhere. North and south it left itself
    whichever way one looked.

Hard to remember now that it's all begun
that it all began and, now that it's all over,
hard to recall it's gone. Those who are gone
arrive in a crest of steam and the late-lamented
    help them with their boxes.

Those to the east have a shed and those to the west
a greenhouse, it was a field and not a field
hereafter, it was a path through new houses
and a sweetshop. There was a lane and another lane
    which, crossing it, was obliged

to name it what it was named and the five things
needed they built buildings for. A meadow
reared its set of gardens like farm-children
edging behind houses to belong there,
    to cluster and imagine

a gate that is always shut will be always open.
But for now the horizon was sky and a blackberry hedge
and the north was the nettle-bed, and the south the roses
and the east an archway to those sad allotments,
    and the west a banded twilight

as out they build, in the time a bedtime story
takes to ferry me shipshape to tomorrow;
out they build till I wake and the horizon's
gone. It won't be found until it's wept to
    on a holiday. The town

is mine, this side of town is mine, the homes
go strolling by, then, bowing out of sight
they scurry round the world to be back in time
for when I pass, as if they never budged,
    and a chuckle of wood-chimes

is all I'll ever know. Now they grow names
with care, they name what dreams of being garden
Garden, what will never be a city
City, and they name it for some hovels
in the Domesday Book. Go where

they say it is. Come to where I'm from.
The north is lost in thought: the glance away
from fairytales is a look through time, the south
is sitting me down and standing me up, the east
unnerves me with its look:

I never heard of west, what's west? and the west
goes west in search of answers. Hard to remember
an hour's walk was a world away across country,
breakfast an age ago. The streets lit up
like anything being thought of

glittered with shame and joy. So I was thought of,
for the north was a copse of houses to be called at,
found wanting at, found wanting *you*, while the south
got London like one gets a belief and beamed
to see it all leads somewhere.

The east I met in dreams was the east I knew
but enormous, so the west escorted me
where those like me *liked* me, on a singing bus-ride
I prayed would never end till I begged it to.
    Things come true, looking back,

things come true I was wishing for, they are gone
and still come true, when north south east and west
flop on a lawn in summer and so do you,
and the time I stare at you and the time you do
    are the same time, are equal,

the same time, same span, like an equals sign
is suddenly loop-the-looping home so it forms
infinity by a hedge in summer – *You,*
I caught your eye in my life. What else did I do?
    and the longer ago it gets

the longer it lasts and closer it seems to come.
Come to where I'll never again be from,
you, there are miracles showing up again
instead of us. The shadows comb the lawn,
    diligent and discreet

as a search team until I call it off
for want of a clue. South go the memories,
north goes love as I wake, while the east and west
welcome the bright apprentice and dispatch him
    daily on his amiable

fruitless errand. My eyes grow books and suffer
books, my ears grow songs and suffer songs,
my hands break news, my feet fetch drinks, my stomach
stomachs it all like something bet it it couldn't,
    and out they build, they build,

from the slim incessant fountain they began with,
to the homes we knew and will never, side by side
they build them, like the ones we won't remember
play tag in the park with the ones we can't forget
    and the kids they brought together

had kids together and soon the north was the poems
I wrote about you, woods of poems I pass through
guided by a voice in headphones, soon
the south is the realm of Alfie Rose, the east
    an airport serving nowhere

and the west the news I brush off like a boy-king
as I stir the foam and find I'm in Manhattan.
And maybe they built out far enough, I wonder,
sipping the wine in a brasserie I always
    loved, or I text my exes

in the terminal or I listen to the songs
I listen to. At the rendezvous of evening
I always miss for mulling over headlines,
what travelled outward travels at standstill,
    then starts to travel in,

when the woodland path arrives in the blue clearing:
the second son of three is getting ready
to set some last adventure with his soldiers.
But his pals who don't take no for an answer shriek
    from the road until he rises,

childhood done forever. The clearing reached,
the path is weeds and litter. Hard to remember,
now I see it all, that it was all I saw,
and I drive through a north I cried in, where the council's
    nailed up signs and arrows

that *These are trees* and *So are these*, and the south
is so far south it's south of understanding,
and the east is the internet and the west my time here
googled with a whisky. Come to where
   I said it was, it's there

I'm gone. The plastic infantryman
dropped in the wood outlasts the wood. I meet you
for the last time but one on a wet Thursday,
and the street rolls up behind me like a script
   unless I turn to stop it.

The fine idea remains just that. The blueprint
flutters down unused, and the children's children
tweet on the ragged swings. There's not a tree,
a yard of light, a lamp-post that won't
   tap from me my only

soliloquy *I remember when we*,
when she, declining, like an old-school verb,
to *when you*. Then you, derailed at a dream-junction,
are someone else again, the old first names
   step out in their parish beauty,

Rosemary, Clare, Diane . . . What I want from one
is what I got from one, as if the maths
made sense in the negative: now writing looks
like black on white but feels like flint on nothing.
    North they are shutting up

the picture book forever, south the theatre's
pricey card for children, east the warehouse
eats the one beside it, west I set out
seats for relatives and replay scenes
    that happened in the west,

right there I mutter, peering into sunset,
pulling a cork among abandoned deck-chairs.
Come to where I'm from, like the bloke I once
got talking to in The Sun, on the only night
    he spent in my birthplace,

a desolate Sunday evening wiping tables
and he said *I hate this town* and he was gone,
said he'd never come again, come again like him,
when you never will, come to where I'm from
    like the glossy editor

at Condé Nast who murmured to me *Glyn,*
it does you no favours, saying where you're from:
say you're 'from Hertfordshire', come again like him,
where you wouldn't be seen dead. Come again like one
    who's lost, come again like one

for seconds on First Capital Connect,
who meant to lift his eyelids from his iPhone
as the little place shot by but when he looks
we're on the Digswell viaduct, gone, bygone,
    high over the green fields

and lanes of where I'm from. The north is a new
flowerbed a stranger tends, the south
four 4x4s on a driveway, from the east
a fellow stops to stare at where we lived
    as if he remembered us

when he lived, I remember him well enough, and the west
is me at work on this by the garden gate.
Preposterous, what was. I watch that gate
for you and all the gone. The odds against
    are stars to sail between.

Come to where I'm from. Now there's nothing here,
hard to remember once there was nothing here.
Hard to remember we paused in a field in sunshine
with a plot for a field and a feel of a place in mind
    and a little knot of horses

faraway in a corner stood right there
near where those horses stand, by the quiet trees,
beyond which all the yellow rising hills
you think are there are the yellow rising hills
    you thought were there.

Homeward Orpheus

He knew he could not come back and he knew he could.
This was a skill they gave him or came up with
bored in eternity and said *Give him that one.*
So he not only thinks both things he knows both things.

He came out of heaven and hell and he knew both things.
One of them bored in eternity sat back
and said *Here's another – heaven and hell are words:*
let him carry their dust on his clogs and still think that.

The rest went *Yeah sounds good.* He reached the world
and women he lost in the past and women he loved
now and women who lost him or loved him now
were in his eyeline, chosen ones he could never

lose again or love again. *He can love them,*
one of them bored in eternity suggested,
but not as before. And they can love him always
but not as before. Okay they will just exist,

remembering stuff. How utterly different from us,
one bored in eternity put it to him in a silence.
That lasted until another one said *But his songs now*
will have to be all about it. Make him play one.

ACKNOWLEDGEMENTS

Acknowledgements are due to the editors of the following
publications in which some of these poems (or versions of them)
first appeared: 'Longinus' and 'Stephaton' (together as 'Two at
the Cross') in *Bat City Review*, 'The Drummers' and 'Homeward
Orpheus' in *Cardinal Points*, 'The Double' and 'This Whiteness'
in *Little Star*, 'Dunwich' in *Magma*, 'The Case of After' in the
New Welsh Review, 'South-East of Eden' in the *New Yorker*,
'Pluto' (as 'Calendar') and 'Birthplace' (as 'Come To Where I'm
From') in *Poetry Review*, and 'The Byelaws', 'Creature of a Play',
'Christmas Seven Times Seven' and 'The Net' (as 'The Furies')
in the *Times Literary Supplement*. 'The Byelaws' was also
published in my critical guidebook *On Poetry* (Oberon Books,
2012); 'Birthplace' was commissioned by the theatre company
Paines Plough for their series of works by playwrights
Come To Where I'm From.